ROME & ROMANS

Heather Amery and Patricia Vanags

Edited by Debbie Martin and Alastair Smith

Designed by Michele Busby, John Jamieson
and Russell Punter

Illustrated by Stephen Cartwright

Contents

IN THE STREETS OF ROME

Look, we've gone back through time. It's about 1,900 years ago and we are in ancient Rome. At this time, Rome is the richest, most important city in all of Europe. It is the capital of a huge empire, made up of the lands that the Romans have conquered. It is full of beautiful buildings, and home to thousands of people.

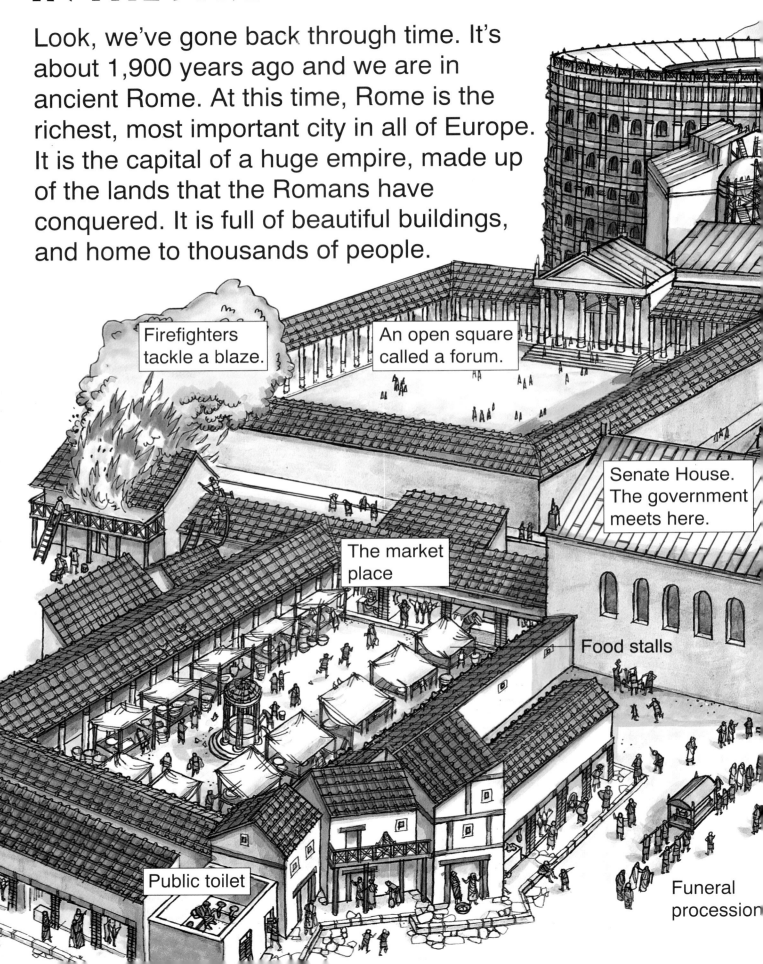

Firefighters tackle a blaze.

An open square called a forum.

Senate House. The government meets here.

The market place

Food stalls

Public toilet

Funeral procession

A huge arena called the Colosseum.

The emperor lives here.

Businessmen meet here.

Temples

Marching soldiers, celebrating a battle victory.

Speeches are given from this platform.

3

AT HOME

This huge house belongs to a rich businessman. Can you see him in his office? Lots of slaves and servants work in his house. They all wear simple brown clothes.

In the middle of the house, there is an open-roofed room. Rainwater falls off its roof into a pool. The pool helps to keep the air cool during hot summer days.

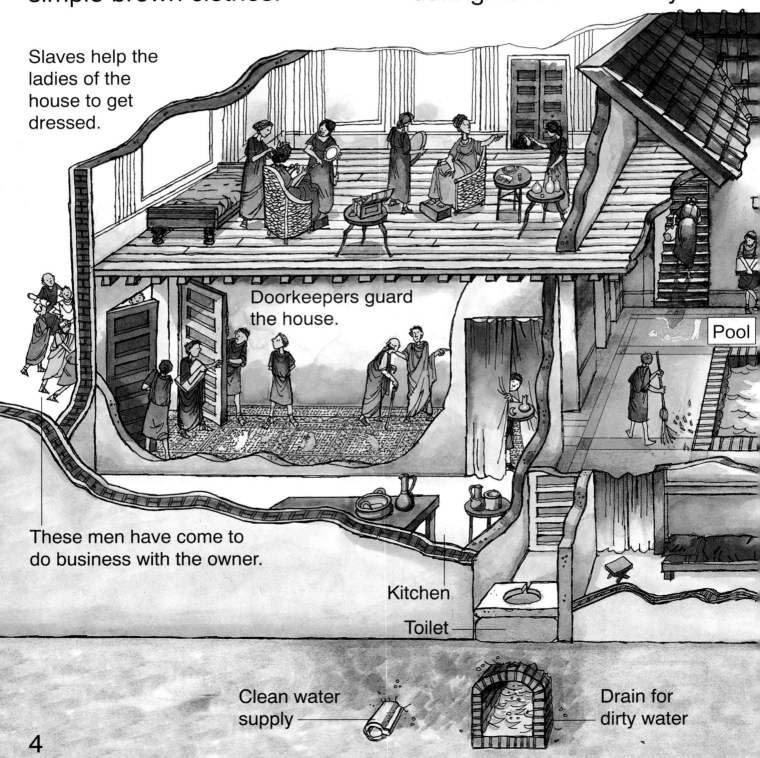

Slaves help the ladies of the house to get dressed.

Doorkeepers guard the house.

Pool

These men have come to do business with the owner.

Kitchen

Toilet

Clean water supply

Drain for dirty water

TOGAS

Roman men are allowed to wear a toga, but slaves and foreigners are not. A toga is a heavy length of woollen cloth. Slaves help their masters to put them on.

This lazy visitor has just woken up.

Assistant

The owner of the house

Office

The eldest son watches his father at work.

Servant's room

Stove

Children's breakfast time

Rich Romans like to decorate their rooms with bright paints.

GOING TO SCHOOL

School begins so early that it is still dark. Can you see a boy carrying a torch to light his way? Children from very rich families don't go to school. They have their lessons at home.

A family lives above the bakery.

Bakery

School for older children.

Teachers are very strict.

This slave is taking a boy to school.

GAMES

After school, the children play games like these.

Hoops

Jacks, played with small bones and a ball.

Games with sticks and balls.

WRITING

Children write by scratching with sticks into boards spread with a coating of wax.

Books are handwritten on rolls of paper, called scrolls. Each end is stuck to a rod.

People write on scrolls using pens made out of small reeds or of a metal called copper.

A naughty boy drawing on a wall.

Schoolmaster

This boy is reciting a poem.

This school is for young children. They learn reading, writing and numbers.

Javelins

Swimming

Mini-chariot racing

GOING SHOPPING

Rome's narrow streets are full of different shops. Many shoppers are slaves, buying food for their owners. Rich people only go shopping for expensive things, such as clothes and jewels.

Food is bought from shops or at the open-air markets. Early each morning, farmers bring food to sell from farms in the country.

Bakery

Oven

This stone mill grinds wheat into flour.

People like to gossip in the streets.

These rich people are choosing some cloth.

Here's a pharmacist treating a patient.

CLEANING CLOTHES

Men called fullers clean togas for rich Romans.

In tubs of water, they stamp all of the dirt out.

Once dried, togas are flattened in a big press.

Slaves collect their masters' clean togas.

THE MARKET

In the square, stalls sell fresh vegetables, fruit, meat and fish.

The markets are bright and lively and are usually packed with people.

This slave is choosing a goose for a feast tonight.

Only rich people can afford meat every day.

This stall sells hot food for people to take away.

AT THE PUBLIC BATHS

Only the richest Romans have bathrooms in their homes, so they go to the public baths to get clean. They can have a hot, steamy bath, a dip in a cold pool, and a relaxing massage. Mostly, men and women go to the baths on different days.

Changing room

The water in here is cold.

Wrestlers

The baths are a good place to meet and chat with friends.

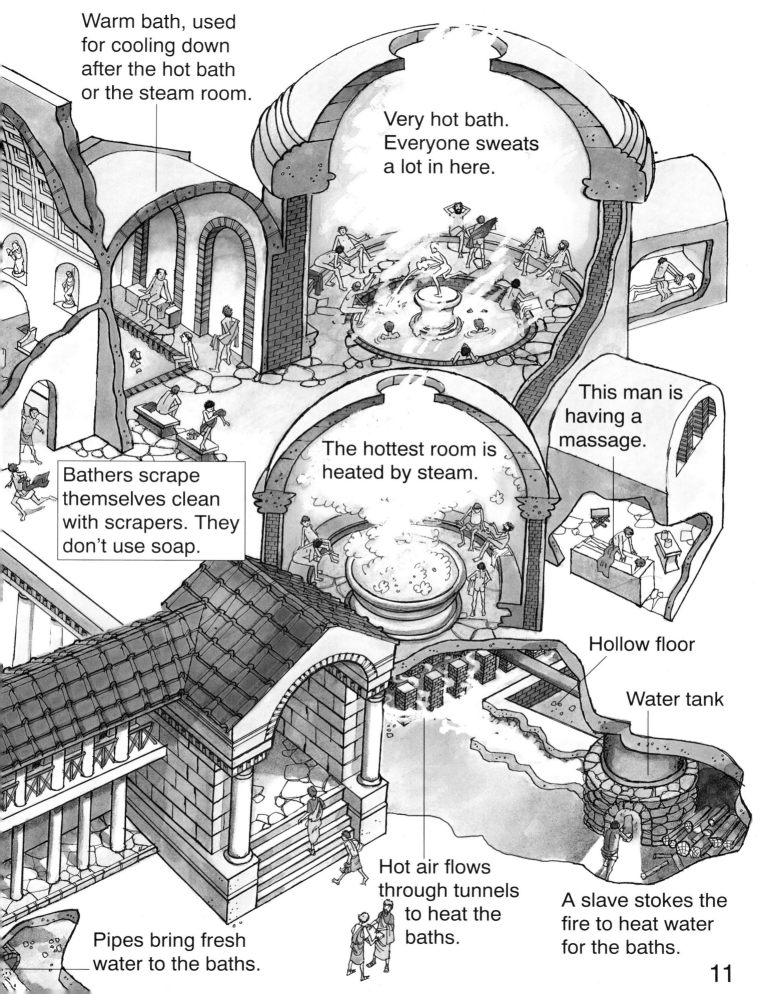

Warm bath, used for cooling down after the hot bath or the steam room.

Very hot bath. Everyone sweats a lot in here.

This man is having a massage.

The hottest room is heated by steam.

Bathers scrape themselves clean with scrapers. They don't use soap.

Hollow floor

Water tank

Hot air flows through tunnels to heat the baths.

Pipes bring fresh water to the baths.

A slave stokes the fire to heat water for the baths.

11

GAMES AND RACES

For a good day out, families go to sports arenas and race tracks. In the arenas, they watch gruesome contests where people and wild animals fight to the death.

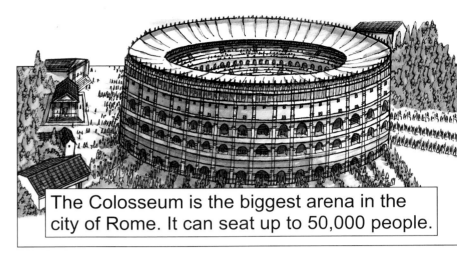

The Colosseum is the biggest arena in the city of Rome. It can seat up to 50,000 people.

Wild animals from all over the empire are brought to fight.

Some of the fighters are specially trained. They are called gladiators. They are really fierce.

GLADIATORS

Gladiators use all sorts of weapons such as nets, spears and swords.

This man flings a heavy net over his opponent to tangle him up.

Wounded gladiators must beg for mercy. The crowd decides their fate.

THE CIRCUS

Chariot races are held at a huge track called the Circus. There are four teams – reds, greens, blues and whites. The winner gets a purse full of gold.

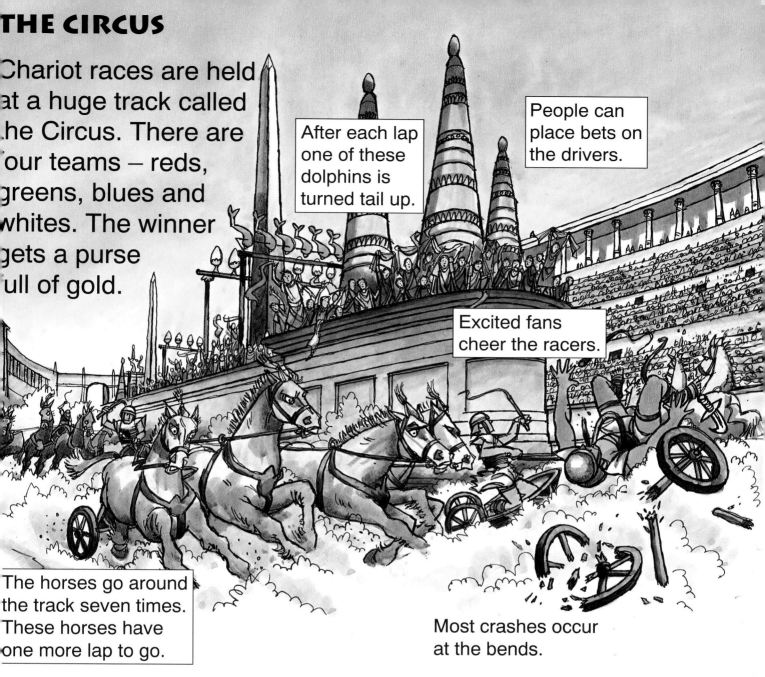

After each lap one of these dolphins is turned tail up.

People can place bets on the drivers.

Excited fans cheer the racers.

The horses go around the track seven times. These horses have one more lap to go.

Most crashes occur at the bends.

A CHARIOT RACE

The racers line up in their light chariots. A trumpet sounds, and they are off.

Charioteers lean back on the reins, which are tied around their waists.

In a crash, the driver must cut the reins to avoid being dragged along.

FEAST TIME

In this rich household a dinner party is being held. In the kitchen, slaves and servants are preparing delicious food. In the dining room the meal has already begun.

Slaves carry this rich guest to the feast in a box called a litter.

This guest is late.

Vegetables are cooked on a stove.

The kitchen is hot, dark and dirty.

These slaves are waiting for their owner.

COOKING

The cook is making a sauce with fish, herbs, spices and honey.

These slaves are chopping up different kinds of vegetables.

Snails are left to fatten in fresh milk. Oysters are eaten live.

THE DINING ROOM

Less important guests eat cheaper food at this table.

Oil lamp

This guest has come with his secretary so he can work while he eats.

Musicians

Slave pouring wine

This poet is waiting to recite poems.

Guests wash their hands between each course.

FIRST COURSE

Stuffed dormice, prunes, peacocks' eggs, olives and an oily sauce.

MAIN COURSE

Deer, ostrich, lobster, dove, boar's head, baby pig and chicken.

THIRD COURSE

Dates, honey cakes, grapes, oranges and other fruits.

INDEX

This book is based on material previously published in
The Usborne Time Traveller Rome and Romans.

First published in 1998 by Usborne Publishing Ltd,
83-85 Saffron Hill, London EC1N 8RT, England.
Copyright © 1998, 1997, 1976 Usborne Publishing Ltd.
The name Usborne and the device ⊕ are Trade Marks of Usborne Publishing Ltd.
All rights reserved. No part of this publication may be reproduced, stored in a retrieval system, or transmitted in
any form or by any means, electronic, mechanical, photocopying, recording or otherwise, without the prior
permission of the publisher. UE.
This edition first published in America in 1999.
Printed in Portugal.